INDEX

Thank you for buying the book! As a token of my gratitude for your support, I have a gift for you: a printable book with 32 original illustrations of player action poses to design your own kits and colour.

I hope you enjoy it!

Thank you for buying the book. AS a token
of my gratitude for your support, I have
a gift for you a printable book with 37
original illustrations of player poses
poses to design your own kits and colour.

I hope you enjoy it

DRAKE LONDON

ATLANTA
FALCONS

9

LAMAR JACKSON

BALTIMORE
RAVENS

BRYCE YOUNG

CAROLINA
PANTHERS

15

JUSTIN FIELDS

CHICAGO
BEARS

18

JOE BURROW

BENGALS

CINCINNATI BENGALS

19

NICK CHUBB

CLEVELAND BROWNS

21

22

28

JORDAN LOVE

GREEN BAY
PACKERS

CJ STROUD

HOUSTON
TEXANS

31

JONATHAN TAYLOR

INDIANAPOLIS
COLTS

33

34

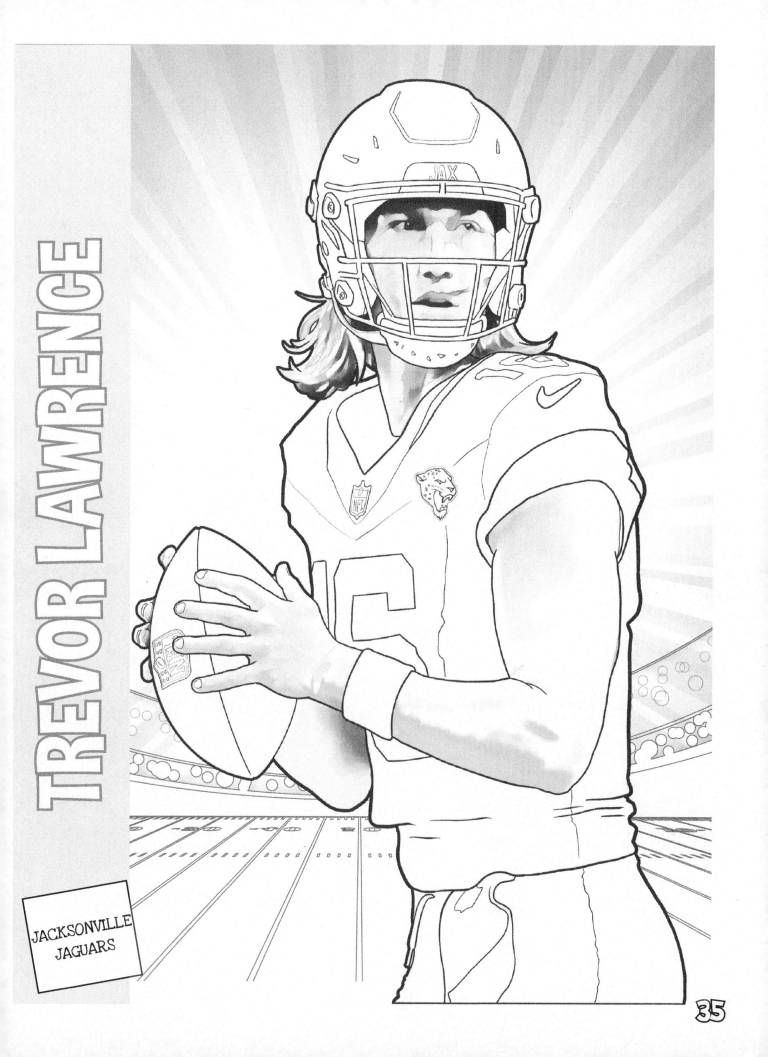

TREVOR LAWRENCE

JACKSONVILLE JAGUARS

35

PATRICK MAHOMES

KANSAS CITY

DAVANTE ADAMS

LAS VEGAS
RAIDERS

39

MATTHEW STAFRFORD

LOS ANGELES RAMS

43

TUA TAGOVAILOA

MIAMI
DOLPHINS

45

46

JUSTIN JEFFERSON

MINNESOTA
VIKINGS

47

RHAMONDRE STEVENSON

NEW ENGLAND PATRIOTS

49

50

DEREK CARR

NEW ORLEANS
SAINTS

SAQUON BARKLEY

NEW YORK
GIANTS

AARON RODGERS

NEW YORK
JETS

T.J. WATT

PITTSBURGH
STEELERS

NICK BOSA

SAN FRANCISCO 49ERS

DK METCALF

SEATTLE
SEAHAWKS

63

TRISTAN WRFS

TAMPA BAY
BUCCANEERS

65

JEFFERY SIMMONS

TENNESSEE TITANS

TERRY MCLAURIN

WASHINGTON
FOOTBALL

69

I hope you enjoyed the book.
If you liked it, leave us a nice review
on Amazon and your comments so
we can keep improving!

We really appreciate your input and
will be happy to implement your
recommendations.

72

Made in the USA
Coppell, TX
09 December 2024

41983895R10044